We Can Use a Map

R. J. MacReady

INFOMAX COMMON CORE READERS

Rosen Classroom™

New York

Published in 2013 by The Rosen Publishing Group, Inc.
29 East 21st Street, New York, NY 10010

Book Design: Michael Harmon

Photo Credits: Cover © iStockphoto.com/ugurhan; p. 4 Monkey Business Images/Shutterstock.com; p. 5 Gorilla/
Shutterstock.com; p. 14 Rob Marmion/Shutterstock.com; p. 16 (lake) David Crausby/Flickr/Getty Images;
p. 16 (path) Jorg Greuel/Digital Vision/Getty Images; p. 16 (street) Manfred Bail/Getty Images.

ISBN: 978-1-4488-8935-8
6-pack ISBN: 978-1-4488-8936-5

Manufactured in the United States of America

CPSIA Compliance Information: Batch #WS12RC: For further information contact Rosen Publishing, New York, New York at 1-800-237-9932.

Word Count:116

Contents

Maps show places in the real world.

We use maps to find our way.

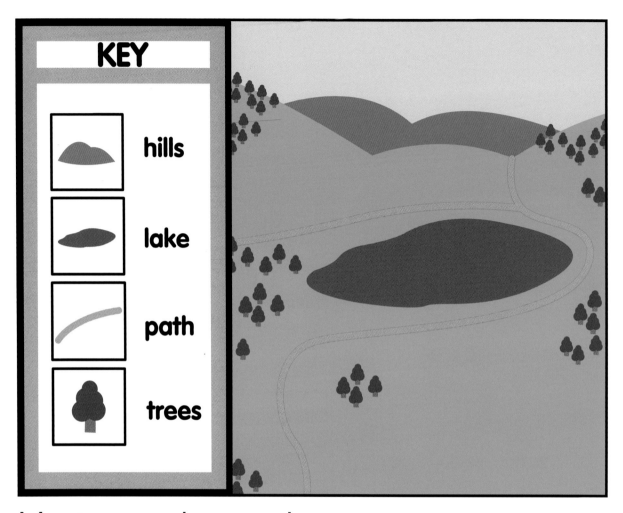

KEY

hills	
lake	
path	
trees	

Most maps have a key.

The key helps us read the map.

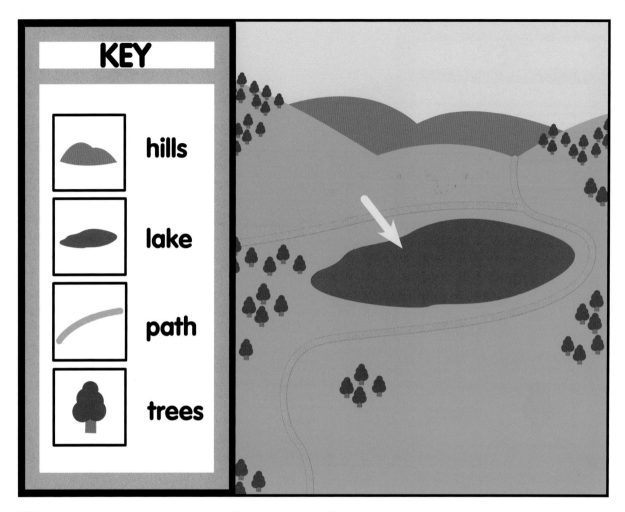

KEY

hills

lake

path

trees

This is a map of a park.

Can you find the lake?

Let's read the map!

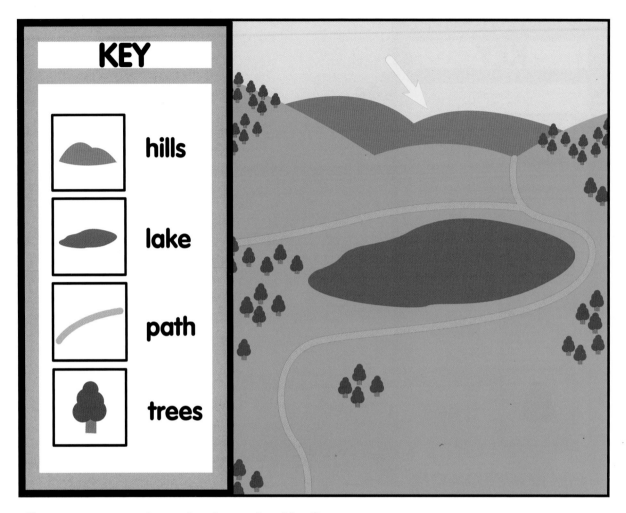

Can you find the hills?

Let's read the map!

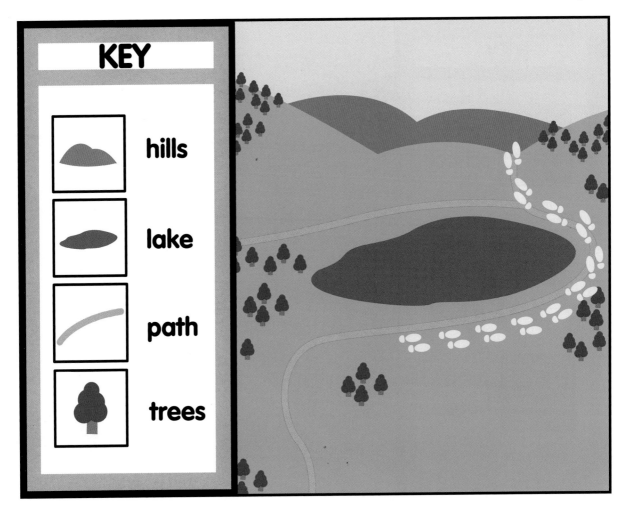

How would you walk from the lake
to the hills?
You would take the path.

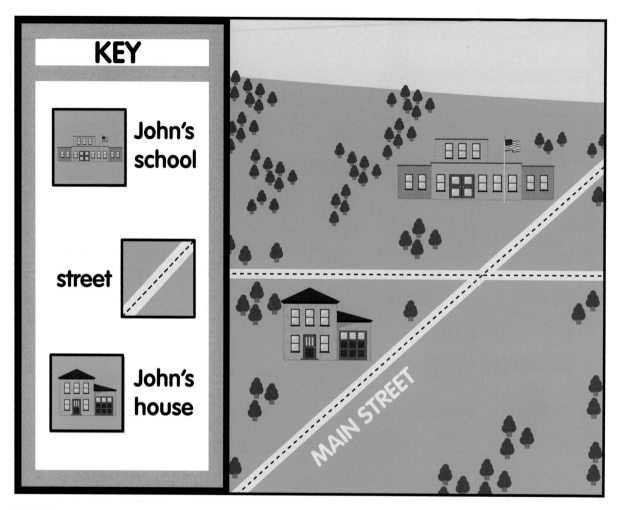

This is a map of the town
where John lives.

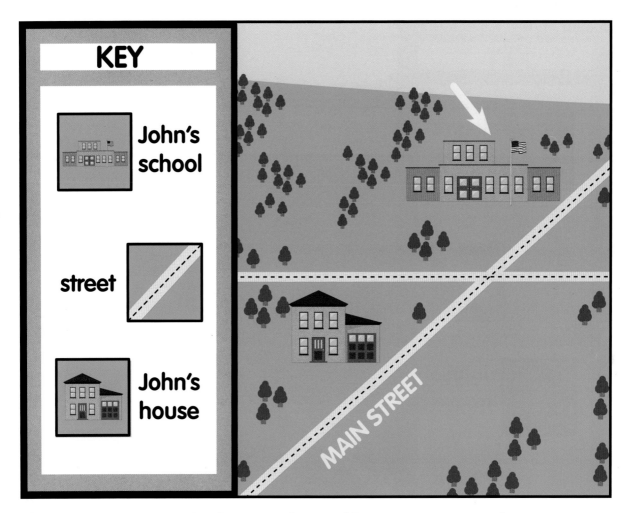

Can you find the school?

Let's read the map!

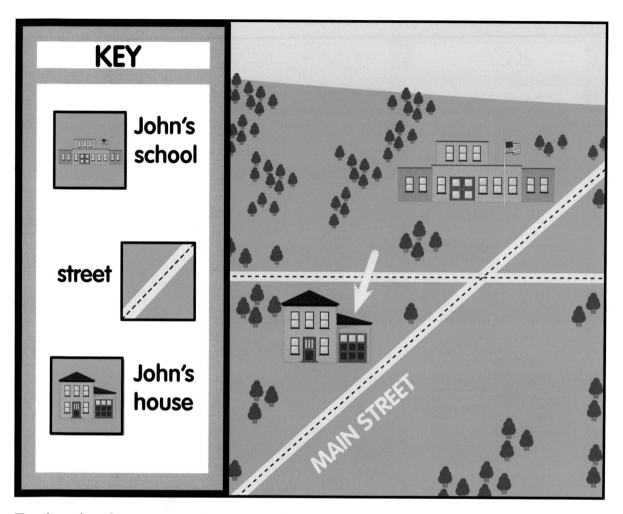

John's house is on the map.

How can John get to the school?

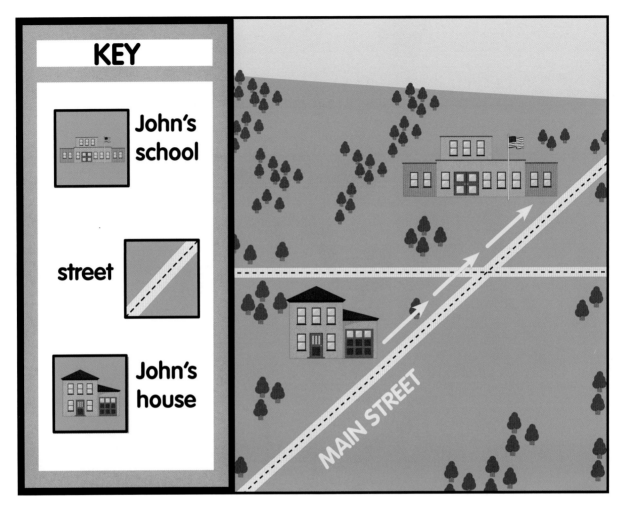

John takes Main Street to the school.

We read the map!

You can even make your own map!

A Map of the Zoo!

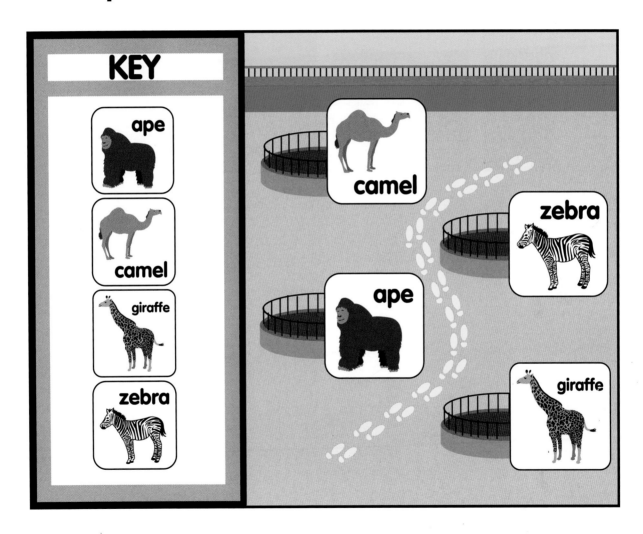

Words to Know

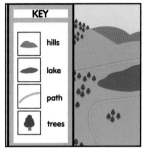
key

lake

path

street

Index